Hello Birdie, Hi Dragonfly!

Coping with grief and loss

By
Lydia Points Martell

Copyright © 2023 by – Lydia Points Martell – All Rights Reserved.

It is not legal to reproduce, duplicate, or transmit any part of this document in either electronic means or printed format. Recording of this publication is strictly prohibited.

Dedications

For my amazing son, Domonic Victor.

Your strength & courage inspires me, may it now inspire others.

I love you – Mom

Acknowledgements

In loving memory of Janet M. Coull, Victor Points, Justin Wright, & Norman Hassan Sr.

"You are loved & missed every day."

About the Author

Lydia Points Martell is a mother & wife from Massachusetts. Lydia's love for writing is almost as strong as her love for her family. Lydia has lost a parent, a grandparent who was like a parent, & a co parent to her child. After all this Lydia learned to grieve while writing. Writing has always been a strong passion of hers. But the most passionate job of all is being a mother. Lydia's son Domonic is her pride & joy.

Hello, birdie; I heard you chirping at my window.

Mama said today's a sad day.

Mama said it's okay to play.

Mama said it's okay to need some space.

Mama said it's okay to go at your own pace.

Mama said it's okay to cry when you're sad.

Mama said it's okay to yell & be mad.

Mama said it's okay to smile too.

So hello, little birdie, I'll smile at you.

Hi Dragonfly, I saw you this morning and now again.

Mama said I've found a friend.

Mama said when you fly by, I can say hi.

So, hi Dragonfly, hi.

Hello birdie, you've come to see me again.

Mama said you're never going away. Mama said it's okay for you to stay.

I love to see you every day; I think today I'll go out & play.

Don't forget, birdie; I'll be back.

So don't go away.

Hello, birdie; I'll be back to smile at you today.

Hi Dragonfly, you fly so high in the sky.

But you always come down to see me.

When I see you, I like to smile.

I hope you'll stick around for a while.

Hello, birdie; today's not a good day.

I don't really want to play.

Mama said it's okay to be sad.

But today I really feel mad.

See, birdie; I want to play with my dad.

But he's not here anymore, so I feel really bad.

But I have you birdie, so I'll smile at you.

Hi Dragonfly, today I feel like crying.

You look so nice when you're around me flying.

But even though I see you, I still feel really blue.

See, my grandma, left, and now Mama wept.

Mama whispered to be strong, but now Mama can't smile for long. Oh, Dragonfly, I need some help right now.

I hope I'll see you again somehow.

Hello, birdie; you seem to make Mama smile.

She looks for you outside the window and says you make her happy for a while.

Hello birdie, you make Mama feel good as new, so I'll smile at you.

Hi Dragonfly, mama said I can talk to you & you will listen.

I don't know what to say; this feels different.

Mama said whatever I want to say to Dad, I can say to you.

Mama said you'd share a message with me too.

Mama said when you're around, I don't need to frown.

Hi Dragonfly, I hope you'll stick around

Hello birdie, today I feel excited.

Mama said I can go back to school.

I missed my friends, especially Billy, he's really cool.

Hello Birdie, I'll be back.

Please don't fly away; Mama wouldn't like that.

Hi Dragonfly, I need you today.

I'm scared a lot.

Can you help me get out this thought?

I want to tell Dad I'm scared without him.

But how will he hear me?

Mama said you're a good listener.

I hope you will tell Dad I was asking for him.

Today I am happy.

I have two friends.

They come to visit me when I am sad, and they even stay when I am mad.

I like to smile when I see them.

They really make my day.

I kind of hope they will stay.

Hello birdie, Hi Dragonfly.

Tell them I miss them and love them so much; it's true.

And when you come back, I'll smile at you.

www.ingramcontent.com/pod-product-compliance
Lightning Source LLC
Chambersburg PA
CBHW041126130526
44590CB00054B/67